Dentists
Help Us

Aaron R. Murray

Enslow Elementary

an imprint of

Enslow Publishers, Inc.
40 Industrial Road
Box 398
Berkeley Heights, NJ 07922
USA

http://www.enslow.com

Enslow Elementary, an imprint of Enslow Publishers, Inc.
Enslow Elementary® is a registered trademark of Enslow Publishers, Inc.

Library of Congress Cataloging-in-Publication Data

Murray, Aaron R.
  Dentists help us / Aaron R. Murray.
    p. cm. — (All about community helpers)
  Includes bibliographical references and index.
  Summary: "Introduces pre-readers to simple concepts about dentits using short sentences and
repetition of words"—Provided by publisher.
  ISBN 978-0-7660-4043-4
  1. Children—Preparation for dental care—Juvenile literature. 2. Dentistry—Juvenile literature.
I. Title.
  RK63.M877 2012
  617.6083—dc23
                              2011031073

Future editions:
Paperback ISBN 978-1-4644-0057-5
ePUB ISBN 978-1-4645-0964-3
PDF ISBN 978-1-4646-0964-0

Printed in the United States of America
032012 Lake Book Manufacturing, Inc., Melrose Park, IL
10 9 8 7 6 5 4 3 2 1

To Our Readers: We have done our best to make sure all Internet Addresses in this book were active
and appropriate when we went to press. However, the author and the publisher have no control over and
assume no liability for the material available on those Internet sites or on other Web sites they may link
to. Any comments or suggestions can be sent by e-mail to comments@enslow.com or to the address on
the back cover.

♻ Enslow Publishers, Inc., is committed to printing our books on recycled paper. The paper in every
book contains 10% to 30% post-consumer waste (PCW). The cover board on the outside of each book
contains 100% PCW. Our goal is to do our part to help young people and the environment too!

Photo Credits: © Brand X, pp. 1, 12, 14, 16, 17; iStockphoto.com: © annedde,
pp. 20–21, © craftvision, pp. 6–7; Shutterstock.com, pp. 1, 3, 4–5, 8, 10, 18, 22, 23.

Cover Photo: Catherine Yeulet/Photos.com

Note to Parents and Teachers
Help pre-readers get a jump-start on reading. These lively stories introduce simple concepts with
repetition of words and short, simple sentences. Photos and illustrations fill the pages with color and
effectively enhance the text. Free Educator Guides are available for this series at www.enslow.com.
Search for the *All About Community Helpers* series name.

Contents

Words to Know

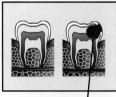  

cavities   mirror   X-ray

A dentist takes care of your teeth and your gums.

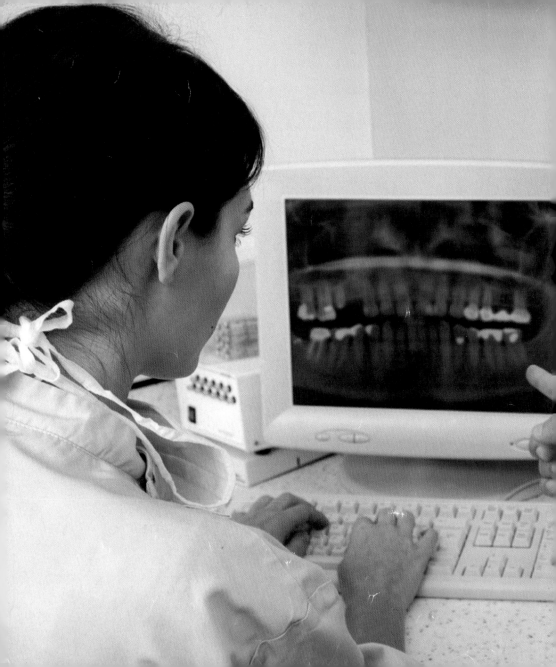

A dentist knows all about teeth and gums.

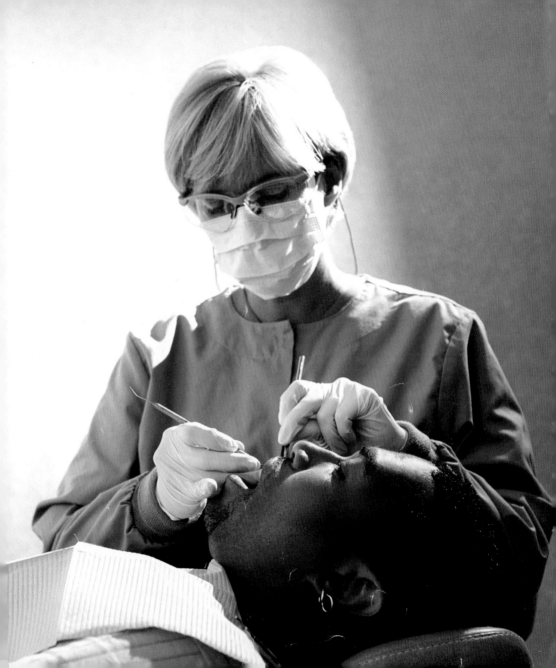

**A dentist uses
lots of tools.**

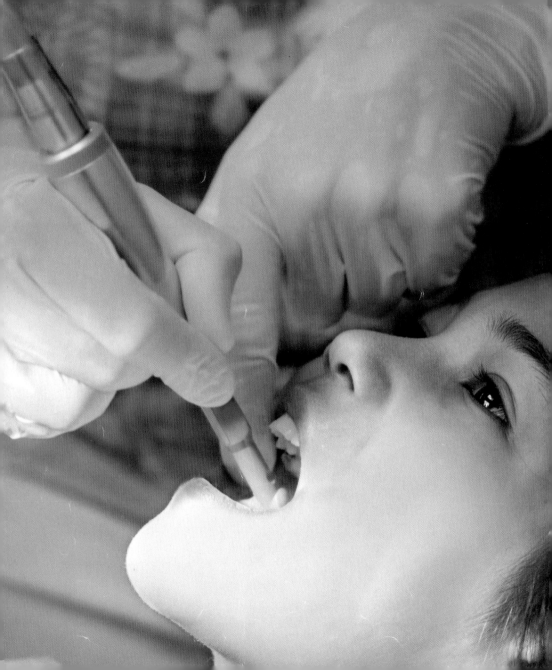

A dentist cleans
your teeth.

A dentist says "Open wide!"

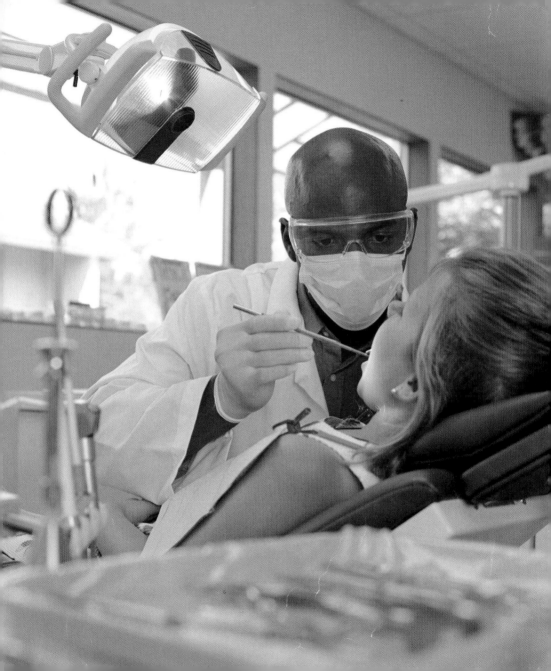

A dentist uses
a little mirror
to see your teeth
and gums.

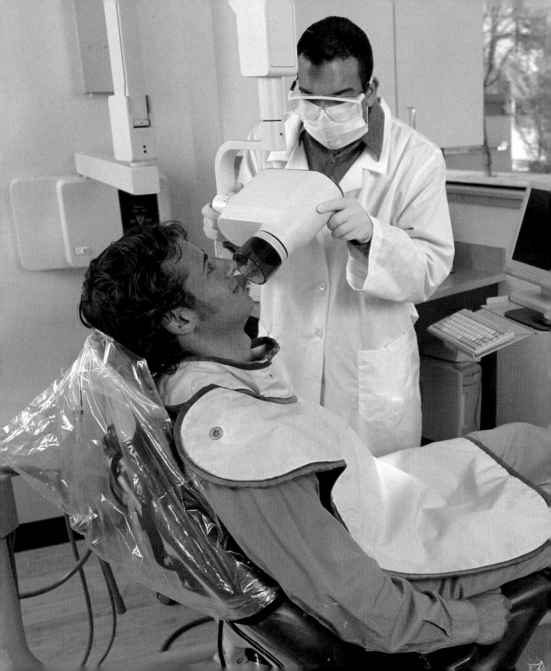

A dentist takes X-rays
of your teeth.

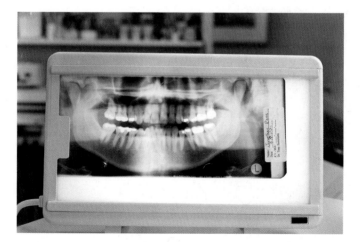

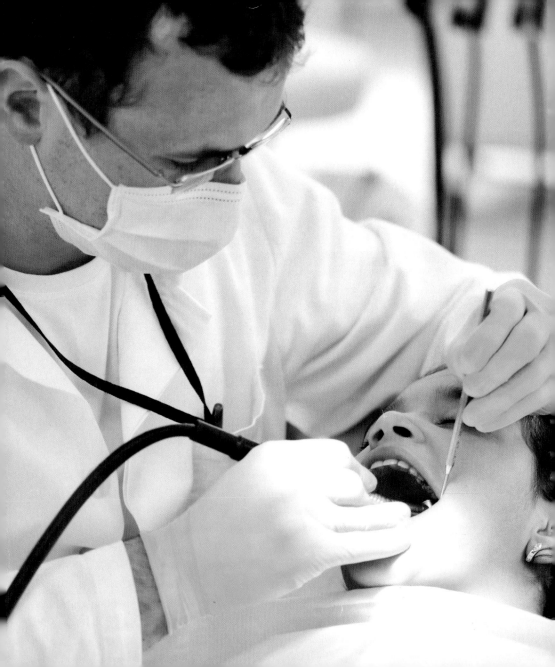

A dentist fixes bad spots on your teeth.

These bad spots are called cavities.

Listen to your dentist.

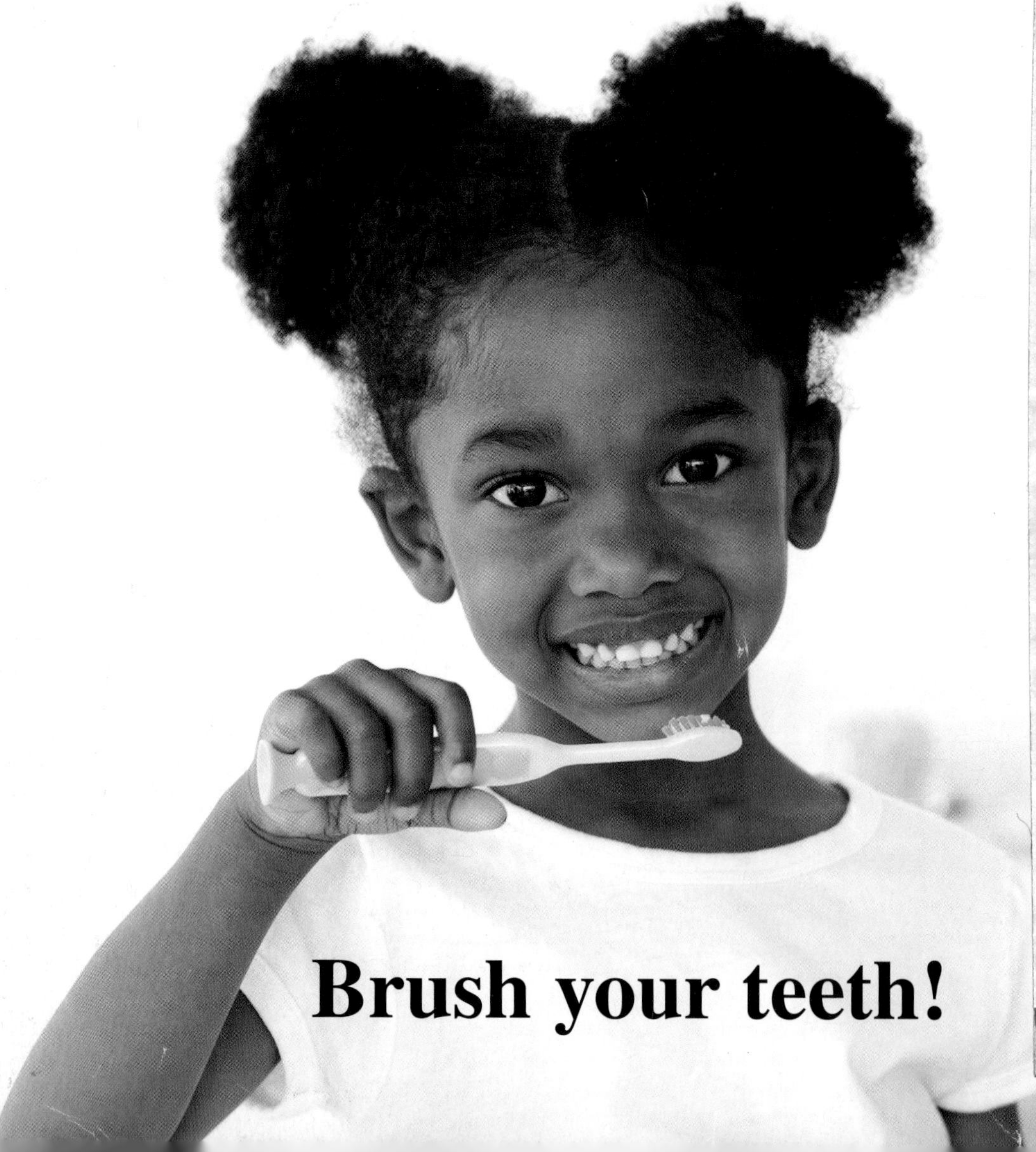

Brush your teeth!

Floss your teeth!

Do you like helping people? You may want to be a dentist.

Read More

Gorman, Jacqueline Laks. *Dentists*. New York: Gareth Stevens Publishing, 2010.

Leake, Diyan. *Dentists*. New York: Heinemann Raintree, 2008.

Miller, Edward. *The Tooth Book: A Guide to Healthy Teeth and Gums*. New York: Holiday House, 2008.

Web Sites

American Dental Hygienists' Association. *Kids Stuff*. <http://www.adha.org/kidstuff/index.html>

Nemours. *KidsHealth*. "Going to the Dentist." <http://kidshealth.org/kid/feel_better/people/go_dentist.html>

Index

Guided Reading Level: C
Guided Reading Leveling System is based on the guidelines recommended by Fountas and Pinnell.

Word Count: 88